ENERGY
RESOURCES

Jack and Meg Gillett
With contributions by Richard and Louise Spilsbury

WAYLAND

Contents

About this book

This book looks at the energy generated around the world to warm houses, power transportation and run factories. It looks at the location and distribution of the various energy resources that so many of us rely on.

The location of a country often determines what natural energy resources it has and how this affects its development. For example, countries with plenty of oil resources have grown rich selling oil to countries with little or no oil.

Today, fossil fuels are the main energy resources in the world. These are finite (will run out one day) and burning them causes pollution and contributes to climate change – the biggest threat to our ecosystems at the present time. However, sustainable energy resources will become more popular in the supply of our energy demands in the future and they will cause less damage to the environment.

Each double page in this book introduces the location and distribution of energy resources in a different region of the world. A map locates relevant sites and graphs and statistics provide important data. At the end of the book is a section you can use for further study and comparisons.

Fun research activity

Map to show the location of the energy resources discussed

Statistical feature for at-a-glance data

Globe shows the location of the map region

Key explains the symbols used in the map

Pictures highlight features discussed or located on the map

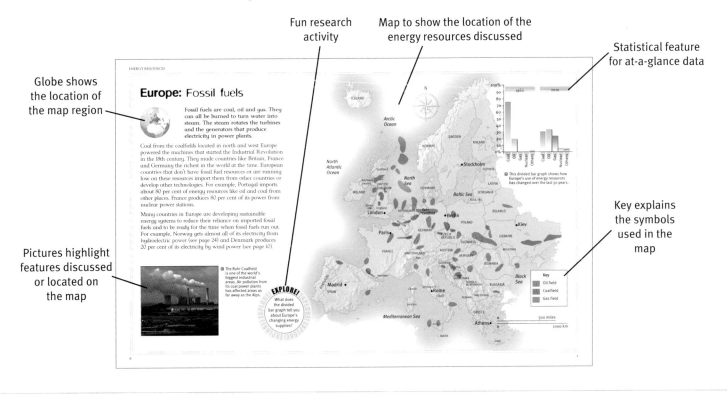

The world: The growing demand for energy

The amount of energy used by the world is constantly increasing. Our total demand for energy is expected to double over the next thirty years.

There are two reasons why the need for energy is increasing worldwide. One is that the world's population rises every year, so there are always more people needing to use energy.

The second reason is that more machines, from mobile phones to cars, are being sold every year, and more energy is needed to make, use and distribute them. This is why places like Europe and North America (see map and table) use more energy per person than a continent like Asia, even though many more people live in Asia.

The table and map also show that Asia is likely to have the biggest population increase and the fastest rise in people's energy needs, for example as more Asians buy cars. These ever-increasing demands for energy means it is vital to find energy resources that are sustainable.

NORTH AMERICA

SOUTH AMERICA

⬆ The Tata Nano, made in India, first came onto the market in 2008. Its low price has made it affordable for many Indians to own a car. This change in lifestyle means that energy demands will rise in India as well.

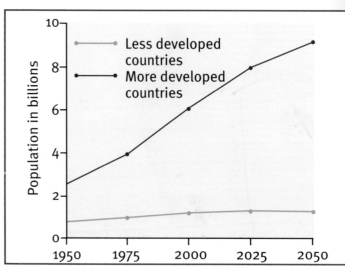

⬆ Every person uses energy, and this line graph shows how the world's population will increase.

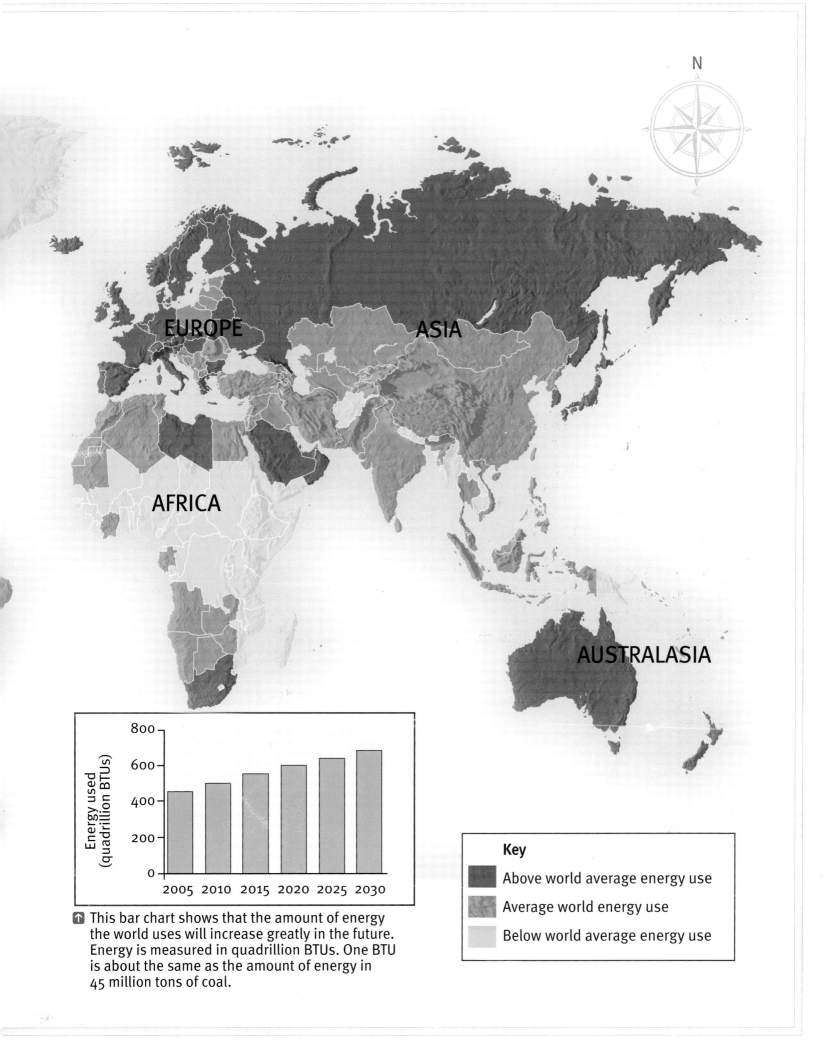

EUROPE

ASIA

AFRICA

AUSTRALASIA

N

Energy used (quadrillion BTUs)

800

600

400

200

0

2005 2010 2015 2020 2025 2030

⬆ This bar chart shows that the amount of energy the world uses will increase greatly in the future. Energy is measured in quadrillion BTUs. One BTU is about the same as the amount of energy in 45 million tons of coal.

Key

Above world average energy use

Average world energy use

Below world average energy use

Europe: Fossil fuels

Fossil fuels are coal, oil and gas. They can all be burned to turn water into steam. The steam rotates the turbines and the generators that produce electricity in power plants.

Coal from the coalfields located in north and west Europe powered the machines that started the Industrial Revolution in the 18th century. They made countries like Britain, France and Germany the richest in the world at the time. European countries that don't have fossil fuel resources or are running low on these resources import them from other countries or develop other technologies. For example, Portugal imports about 80 per cent of energy resources like oil and coal from other places. France produces 80 per cent of its power from nuclear power stations.

Many countries in Europe are developing sustainable energy systems to reduce their reliance on imported fossil fuels and to be ready for the time when fossil fuels run out. For example, Norway gets almost all of its electricity from hydroelectric power (see page 24) and Denmark produces 20 per cent of its electricity by wind power (see page 10).

North Atlantic Ocean

IRELAND

← The Ruhr Coalfield is one of the world's biggest industrial areas. Air pollution from its coal power plants has affected areas as far away as the Alps.

PORTUGAL

Madrid ●

SPAIN

EXPLORE!

What does the divided bar graph tell you about Europe's changing energy supplies?

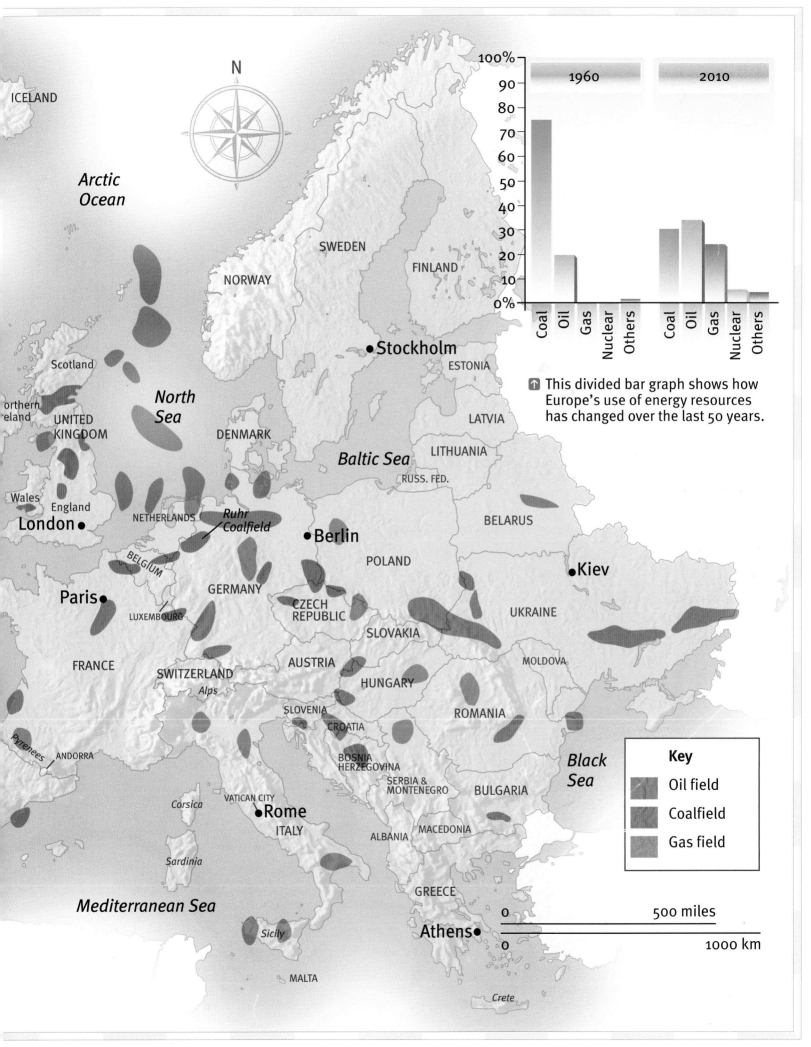

ICELAND

Arctic
Ocean

N

SWEDEN

NORWAY

FINLAND

● Stockholm

ESTONIA

Scotland

North
Sea

LATVIA

Northern
Ireland

UNITED
KINGDOM

DENMARK

Baltic Sea

LITHUANIA

RUSS. FED.

Wales

England

London ●

NETHERLANDS

Ruhr
Coalfield

● Berlin

BELARUS

BELGIUM

POLAND

● Kiev

Paris ●

LUXEMBOURG

GERMANY

CZECH
REPUBLIC

SLOVAKIA

UKRAINE

FRANCE

SWITZERLAND

Alps

AUSTRIA

HUNGARY

MOLDOVA

SLOVENIA

CROATIA

ROMANIA

Pyrenees

ANDORRA

BOSNIA
HERZEGOVINA

Black
Sea

Corsica

VATICAN CITY

SERBIA &
MONTENEGRO

BULGARIA

● Rome

ITALY

ALBANIA

MACEDONIA

Sardinia

GREECE

Mediterranean Sea

Sicily

Athens ●

MALTA

Crete

Key

Oil field

Coalfield

Gas field

0 ————— 500 miles

0 ————— 1000 km

100%
90
80
70
60
50
40
30
20
10
0%

1960   2010

Coal | Oil | Gas | Nuclear | Others   Coal | Oil | Gas | Nuclear | Others

⬆ This divided bar graph shows how
Europe's use of energy resources
has changed over the last 50 years.

7

Europe: Wave and tidal power

Wave and tidal power are both generated by the sea. Wave power uses the movement of the water surface. Tidal power is generated using the movement of water between high and low tides. Europe has a long coastline, which makes it ideal for generating both types of energy.

Europe leads the world in wave and tidal technology. The world's first tidal power station was built in France in 1966 and the world's first wave power plant was built in 2008 at the Agucadoura Wave Park in Portugal. New wave and tidal plants are planned for the future, for example a new tidal power station in Scotland in 2011.

These technologies do not provide Europe with all of its energy needs at present. Countries in Europe also use other forms of sustainable energy such as solar, wind and hydroelectric power. Energy companies in Europe hope to share renewable electricity in a 'Supergrid' in future. This would allow countries with wave power stations to import wind power from windier regions to fulfil their energy needs.

⬆ The world's first tidal power station was built across the La Rance river, in northern France.

ICELAND

N

North Atlantic Ocean

Scotland

Northern Ireland

IRELAND

UNITED KINGDOM

Wales | England

London

La Rance tidal power station

Paris

FRA

PORTUGAL

Agucadoura Wave Park

Pyrenees

ANDORR

Madrid

SPAIN

0   500 miles

0   1000 km

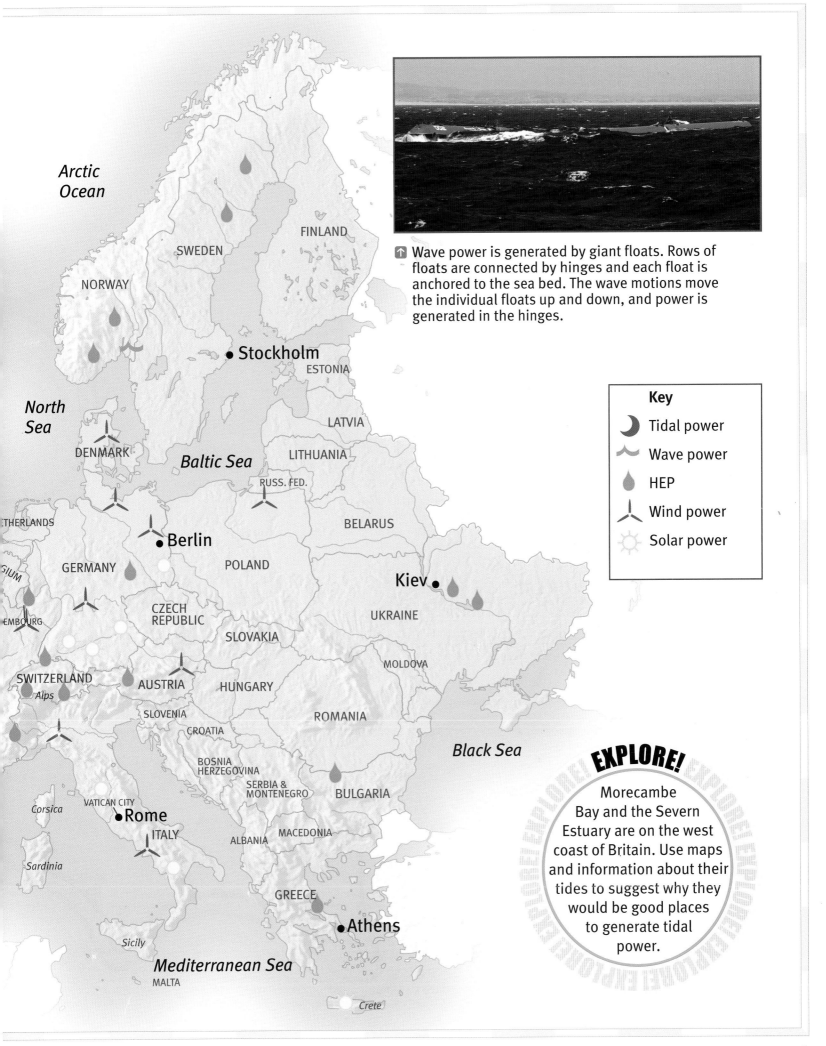

Arctic
Ocean

FINLAND

SWEDEN

NORWAY

Wave power is generated by giant floats. Rows of floats are connected by hinges and each float is anchored to the sea bed. The wave motions move the individual floats up and down, and power is generated in the hinges.

● **Stockholm**

ESTONIA

North
Sea

LATVIA

DENMARK

Baltic Sea

LITHUANIA

RUSS. FED.

Key

◗ Tidal power

〰 Wave power

◗ HEP

✶ Wind power

☼ Solar power

NETHERLANDS

BELARUS

● **Berlin**

GERMANY

POLAND

Kiev ●

:GIUM

EMBOURG

CZECH
REPUBLIC

UKRAINE

SLOVAKIA

SWITZERLAND

AUSTRIA

HUNGARY

MOLDOVA

Alps

SLOVENIA

ROMANIA

CROATIA

Black Sea

BOSNIA
HERZEGOVINA

SERBIA &
MONTENEGRO

BULGARIA

Corsica

VATICAN CITY

● **Rome**

MACEDONIA

ITALY

ALBANIA

Sardinia

GREECE

Sicily

● **Athens**

Mediterranean Sea

MALTA

Crete

EXPLORE!

Morecambe Bay and the Severn Estuary are on the west coast of Britain. Use maps and information about their tides to suggest why they would be good places to generate tidal power.

The British Isles:
Wind power

Wind power is generated by turbines such as the ones in the photograph below. The British Isles are affected by strong south-westerly and north-easterly winds. This makes it an ideal location for wind power generation.

Wind turbines are usually built in clusters, called wind farms. The best sites for wind farms are offshore, or hilltops where strong winds blow. Some people complain that turbines' blades are noisy and that turbines spoil the scenery. Many believe that they are better for the environment than power stations burning fossil fuels.

In the past, Britain relied on coal, gas and oil, and nuclear power since the 1950s. This is set to change. Fossil fuels are running out and nuclear plants are unpopular with many people, so the British government is giving people grants to fit small wind turbines to buildings and paying farmers to provide land for wind turbines. Many British politicians believe wind turbines could power the equivalent of all Britain's homes in future, even though they cannot generate electricity on calm days.

EXPLORE! Find out where the nearest wind farm to your own house is. How many wind turbines does it have? It is on the coast? Is it on high land?

Key

	Oil field
	Coalfield
	Gas field
	Wind power
	Wave power
	Nuclear power
	Oil pipeline
	Gas pipeline
	Borders of oil and gas exploration areas

⬆ This wind farm is on a ridge of high land near Halifax, in West Yorkshire. It is exposed to winds blowing from all directions.

Kinds of wind farm locations in Britain	Per cent of wind farms in each kind of location
Offshore	26
On islands	7
On the west coast	31
On the east coast	7
All other locations	29

⬆ Most of Britain's wind farms are in places that are exposed to the strong winds blowing off the Atlantic Ocean.

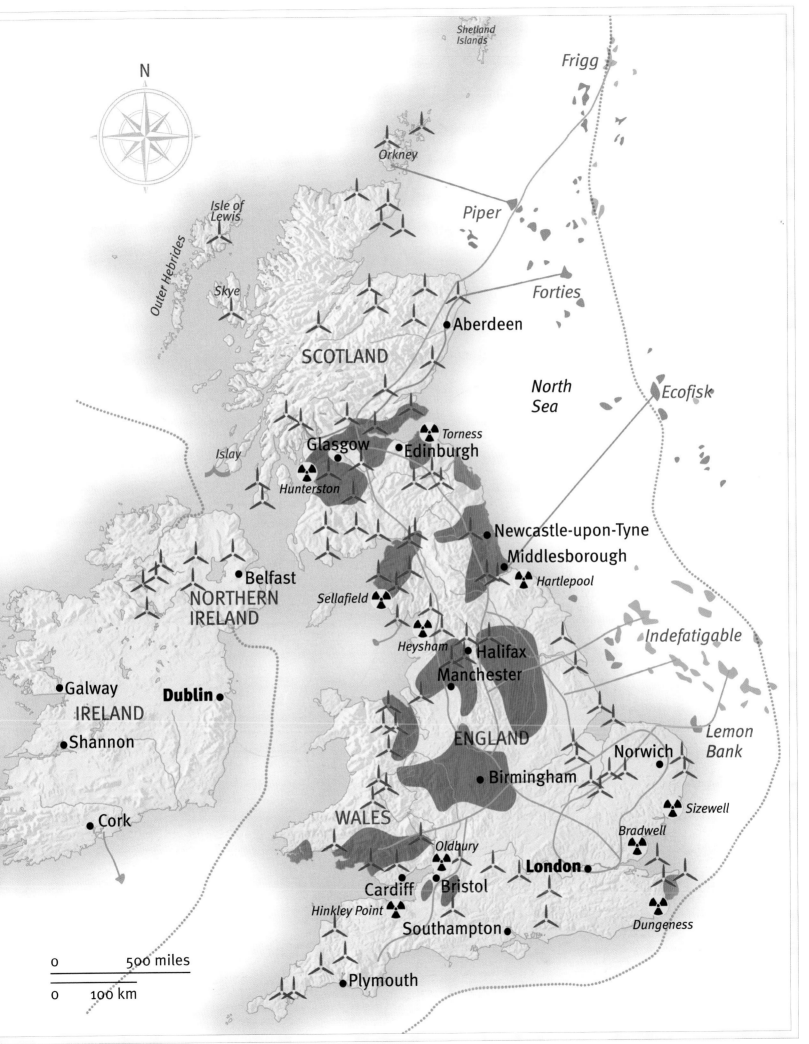

N

Russian Federation and Kazakhstan: Gas

Gas is the decayed remains of tiny sea creatures that lived over 200 million years ago and are now trapped in layers of porous rock.

Gas is a popular form of energy because it is easily ignited, giving instant heat. It also doesn't pollute the air as much as coal, and burning it doesn't produce any ash. However, gas is a fossil fuel, which means that it is finite and so will eventually run out.

The Russian Federation and Kazakhstan are rich in energy resources, including oil and gas, which are sometimes found in the same regions. This is because both are trapped in porous rocks, which have millions of tiny holes (called pores) in them and occur in rock basins. These basins can be several hundred kilometres wide.

Although this doesn't appear so on the map, Russia and Kazakhstan have over 30 per cent of the world's total reserves of gas. Much of it is exported to the densely-populated countries of Western Europe. This is done using pipelines – a cheap and efficient way of transporting gases and liquids.

Key

- Oil field
- Coalfield
- Gas field
- Oil pipeline
- Gas pipeline

EXPLORE!

Using the map, work out how many kilometres gas from northern Russia has to travel to reach Scotland.

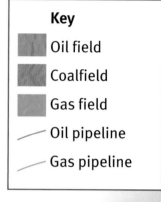

North Atlantic Ocean

North Sea

IRELAND

UNITED KINGDOM

London •

NETH

BEL

Paris •

Seine

Loire

FRANCE

Ebro

PORTUGAL

Tagus

• Madrid

SPAIN

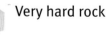

→ This diagram shows a typical cross-section through a basin of porous rocks containing oil and gas.

Very hard rock

Porous rock containing gas

Porous rock containing oil

Porous rock containing water

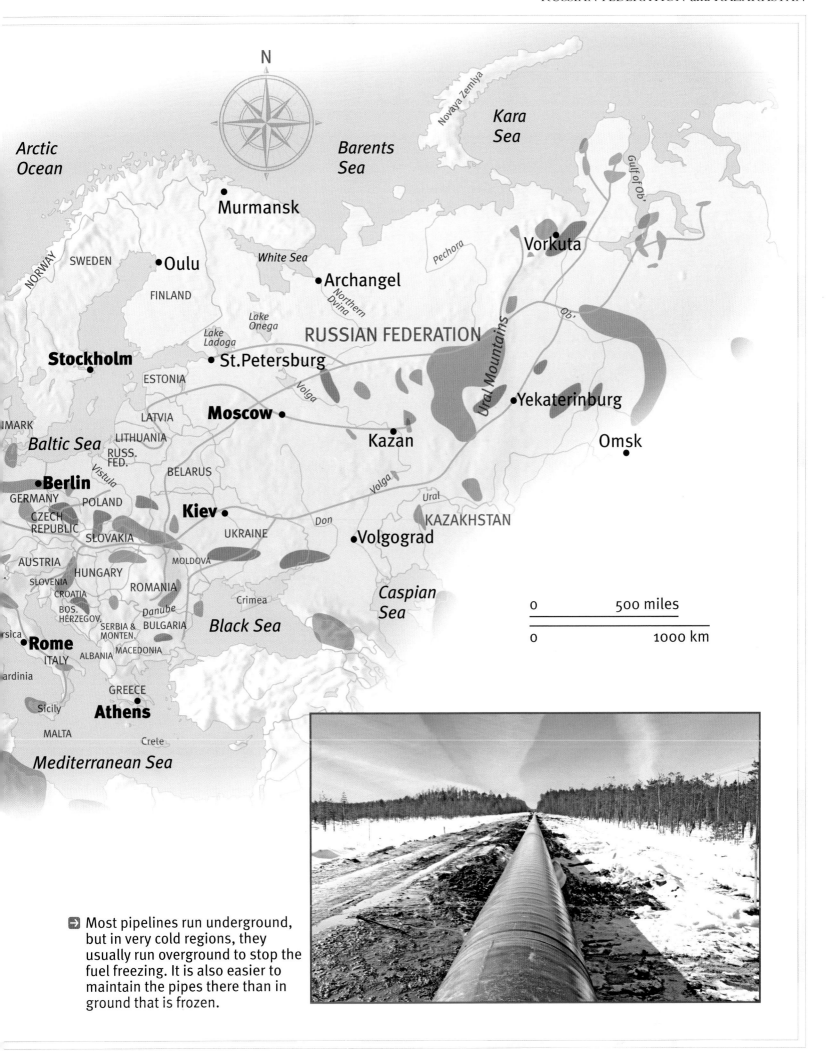

N

Arctic Ocean

Barents Sea

Kara Sea

Novaya Zemlya

Gulf of Ob'

Murmansk

SWEDEN

NORWAY

•Oulu

White Sea

FINLAND

•Archangel

Pechora

Vorkuta

Northern Dvina

Lake Onega

Lake Ladoga

RUSSIAN FEDERATION

Ural Mountains

Ob'

Stockholm

ESTONIA

•St.Petersburg

Volga

•Yekaterinburg

LATVIA

Moscow •

Kazan

Omsk

Baltic Sea

LITHUANIA

RUSS. FED.

IMARK

Vistula

BELARUS

•Berlin

GERMANY

POLAND

Volga

Ural

CZECH REPUBLIC

SLOVAKIA

Kiev •

UKRAINE

Don

KAZAKHSTAN

AUSTRIA

HUNGARY

MOLDOVA

•Volgograd

SLOVENIA

CROATIA

ROMANIA

Crimea

Caspian Sea

BOS. HERZEGOV.

Danube

SERBIA & MONTEN.

BULGARIA

Black Sea

rsica

•Rome

ALBANIA

MACEDONIA

ITALY

ardinia

GREECE

Sicily

Athens

MALTA

Crete

Mediterranean Sea

0	500 miles
0	1000 km

➡ Most pipelines run underground, but in very cold regions, they usually run overground to stop the fuel freezing. It is also easier to maintain the pipes there than in ground that is frozen.

The Middle East: Oil

Oil has to be processed before it can be used. This takes place in refineries, which are usually on the coast. The oil is carried there in huge ships, called supertankers, or piped ashore.

Many of the world's largest oil reserves are found in extreme environments like deserts and stormy seas. Many of the Middle East's oilfields are in hot deserts or in The Gulf. It is expensive to explore for oil and drill hundreds of deep wells in these places. However, oil is a valuable resource, especially now that other regions such as Europe are running out of it, so some Middle Eastern countries have become very rich by exporting it. Some are so rich that their people now have free telephone and medical services!

The economy of the Middle East relies heavily upon oil exports to America, Asia and Europe. For example, in Saudi Arabia three-quarters of government money comes from selling oil and Iran earns about 60 per cent of its income from oil exports. However, like all fossil fuels, oil is a finite resource and may run out in the Middle East by 2090, so some countries are developing sustainable power sources. Iran is building wind farms and solar power plants to make use of the many hours of sunlight in the region and Abu Dhabi is building the largest single solar power plant in the world.

EXPLORE!
Investigate what kinds of by-products are made from oil.

Syria
Dese

Sakākah •

• Tabūk

Umm Lajj •

Medin

Yanbu 'al Bahr •

Jedda •
Mecca

Red Sea

⬅ One of the many oil wells that make Saudi Arabia the world's biggest producer of oil.

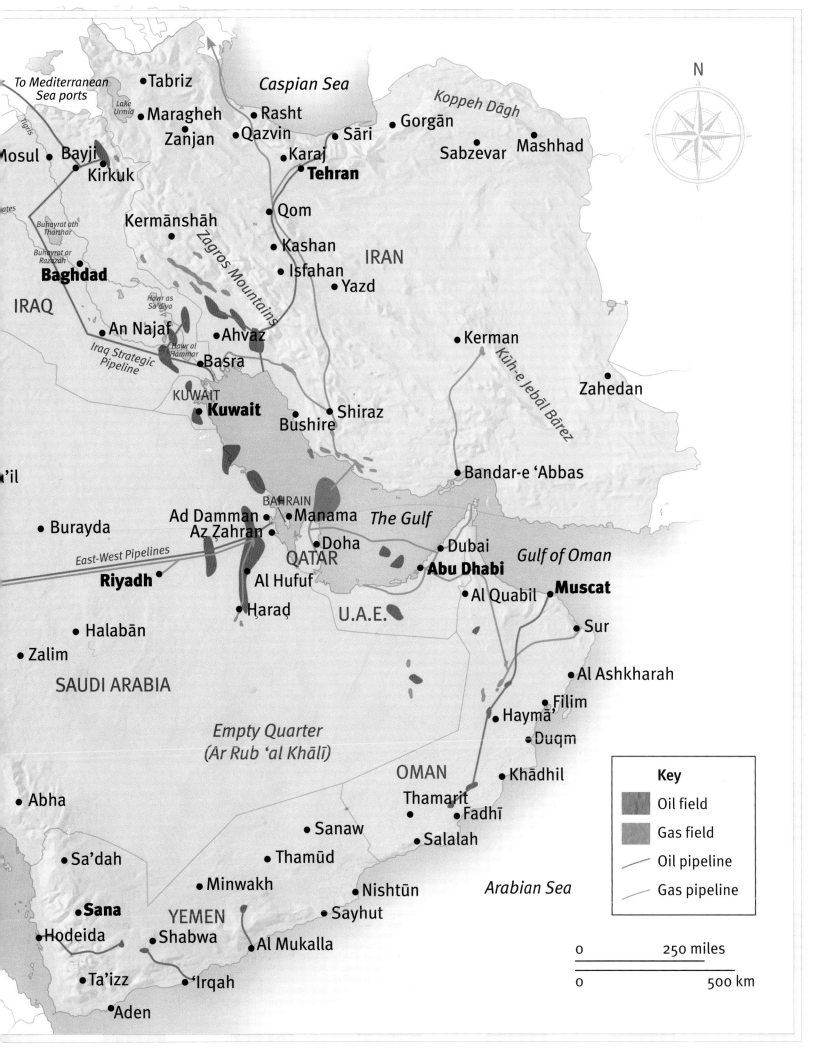

N

To Mediterranean
Sea ports

Tigris

Mosul • Bayji
• **Kirkuk**

Euphrates

*Buhayrat ath
Tharthar*

*Buhayrat ar
Razazah*

Baghdad •

IRAQ

*Hawr as
Sa'diya*

• An Najaf

*Iraq Strategic
Pipeline*

*Hawr al
Hammar*

• Basra

KUWAIT

Kuwait •

• Tabriz

*Lake
Urmia*

• Maragheh
Zanjan

• Kermānshāh

Caspian Sea

• Rasht
• Qazvin   • Sāri
• Karaj

Tehran •

• Qom

• Kashan

Zagros Mountains

• Isfahan

• Ahvaz

Bushire

• Shiraz

• Gorgān

Sabzevar

Koppeh Dāgh

• Mashhad

IRAN

• Yazd

• Kerman

Kūh-e Jebāl Bārez

• Zahedan

• Bandar-e 'Abbas

BAHRAIN

Ad Damman •   • Manama

• Burayda

Az Zahran •

East-West Pipelines

Riyadh •

• Halabān

• Zalim

SAUDI ARABIA

• Abha

The Gulf

• Doha

QATAR

Al Hufuf

• Haraḍ

U.A.E.

*Empty Quarter
(Ar Rub 'al Khālī)*

• Sa'dah

Sana •

• Hodeida   • Shabwa

• Ta'izz   • 'Irqah

• Aden

YEMEN

• Dubai

• Abu Dhabi

Gulf of Oman

• Al Quabil

• Muscat

• Sur

• Al Ashkharah

• Filim
Haymā' •
• Duqm

OMAN

• Khādhil

Thamarit
•   • Fadhī

• Sanaw   • Salalah

• Thamūd

• Minwakh

Arabian Sea

• Nishtūn

• Sayhut

• Al Mukalla

Key	
▮	Oil field
▮	Gas field
—	Oil pipeline
—	Gas pipeline

0 ——————— 250 miles

0 ——————— 500 km

India: Biomass energy

Biomass energy is mainly produced from fuelwood, crop left-overs and cattle dung. Biomass plants use these materials to produce gas, which can then be used for heating and generating electricity for lighting homes and streets.

India is an ideal location for biomass energy plants because the country has many forests and a lot of its population are subsistence farmers, so there are plentiful supplies of dung and crop left-overs. Biomass is also an ideal fuel because many Indian villages are in such remote locations that they cannot receive electricity from the main grid. The Biomass Energy for Rural India project was founded in 2001 to provide remote villages with biomass technology and teach them how to produce their own electricity sustainably.

Kasai was one of the first villages in India to have a biomass energy plant. It uses fuel from woodland nearby, which is managed sustainably to ensure a constant supply of wood to make electricity. Villagers use this power supply for cooking, lighting and heating, but they are also buying more electrical machines like TVs, music systems and computers so the amount of energy they use has greatly increased.

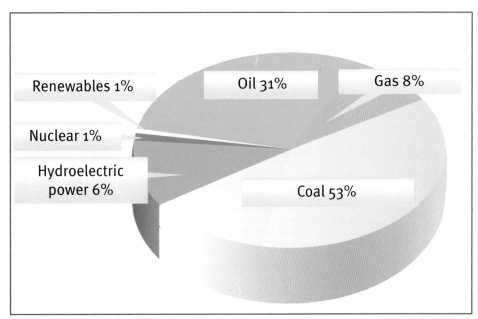

Renewables 1%

Oil 31%

Gas 8%

Nuclear 1%

Hydroelectric power 6%

Coal 53%

⬆ This pie graph shows how the electricity was used for India's first village biomass generator, at Hosahalli.

⬆ The biomass plant in Kasai is maintained by one of the villagers, who has had training to do this work.

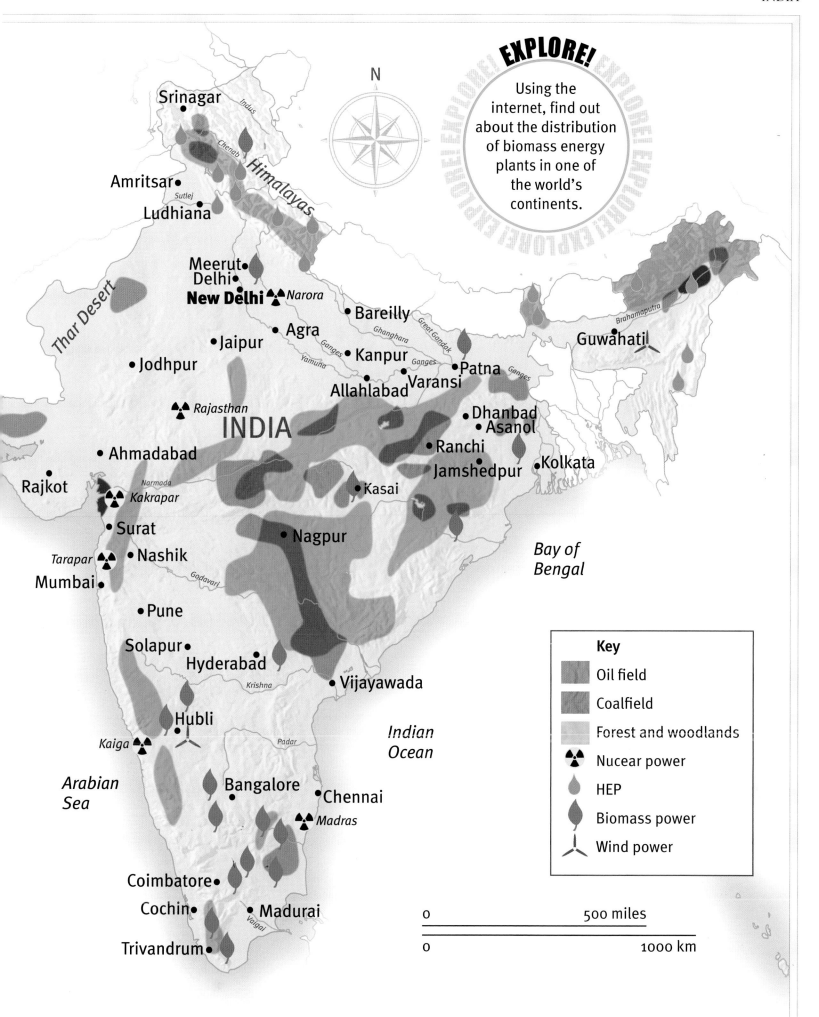

EXPLORE!

Using the internet, find out about the distribution of biomass energy plants in one of the world's continents.

Srinagar

Indus

Chenab

Himalayas

N

Amritsar

Sutlej

Ludhiana

Meerut
Delhi

New Delhi *Narora*

Bareilly

Agra

Ghanghara

Great Gandak

Guwahati

Brahamaputra

Jaipur

Ganges

Kanpur

Ganges

Jodhpur

Yamuna

Patna

Ganges

Varansi

Allahlabad

Thar Desert

Rajasthan

INDIA

Dhanbad
Asanol

Ahmadabad

Ranchi

Jamshedpur

Kolkata

Rajkot

Narmada

Kakrapar

Kasai

Surat

Bay of
Bengal

Tarapar

Nashik

Godavari

Mumbai

Nagpur

Pune

Solapur

Hyderabad

Krishna

Vijayawada

Indian
Ocean

Hubli

Padar

Kaiga

Arabian
Sea

Bangalore

Chennai

Madras

Coimbatore

Cochin

Madurai

Vaigai

Trivandrum

Key

Oil field

Coalfield

Forest and woodlands

Nucear power

HEP

Biomass power

Wind power

0 — 500 miles

0 — 1000 km

China: Coal

Coal is the decayed remains of ancient forests, which have been compressed into solid rock over the last 350 million years. Coal has many uses, including generating electricity in power stations and melting iron ore in steelworks. It is also the raw material for many products that we use in everyday life.

China is the world's biggest producer and user of coal. China's coal fields are located in the east, so large amounts of it have to be transported long distances to provide the rest of the country with energy. The location of the coalfields is also the reason that 60 per cent of China's industries are in the east, including many of the steel factories that make China the biggest steel producing country in the world.

China's success in industry means more people can afford to buy more goods and this has increased the country's energy consumption. At present, coal provides about two-thirds of China's power, but it is also developing new hydroelectric plants, such as the Three Gorges Dam, which is the largest in the world.

⬆ Coal-fired power stations can cause serious air pollution, like here in Guangzhou City, China. The more modern power stations can filter out most of the smoke before it leaves the chimney.

KEY

▨ Oil field

▨ Coalfield

▨ Gas field

⬥ HEP

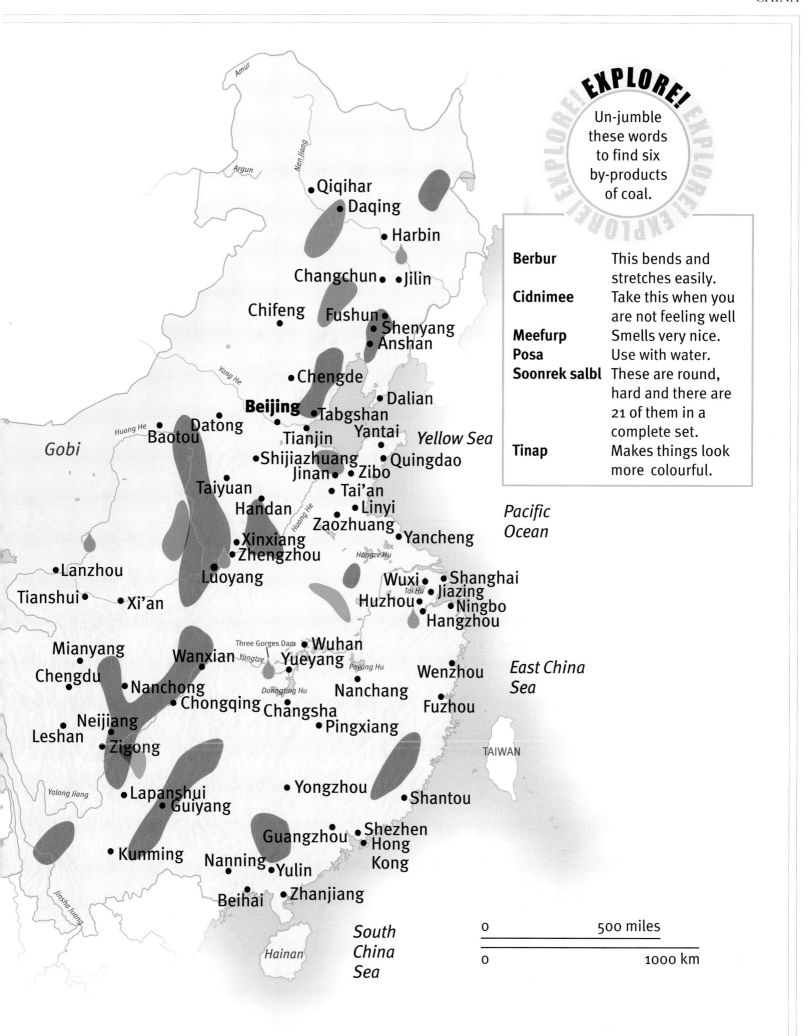

EXPLORE!

Un-jumble these words to find six by-products of coal.

Berbur	This bends and stretches easily.
Cidnimee	Take this when you are not feeling well
Meefurp	Smells very nice.
Posa	Use with water.
Soonrek salbl	These are round, hard and there are 21 of them in a complete set.
Tinap	Makes things look more colourful.

Amur

Nen Jiang

Argun

• Qiqihar
• Daqing
• Harbin
Changchun • Jilin
Chifeng • Fushun
• Shenyang
• Anshan

Yang He

• Chengde
• Dalian
Beijing • Tabgshan
Huang He Datong
Baotou Tianjin Yantai *Yellow Sea*
Gobi • Shijiazhuang
Jinan • Zibo • Quingdao
Taiyuan • Tai'an
Handan • Linyi *Pacific*
Huang He Zaozhuang *Ocean*
• Xinxiang • Yancheng
• Zhengzhou
• Lanzhou Luoyang *Hongze Hu*
Tianshui • Wuxi • Shanghai
• Xi'an *Tai Hu* • Jiazing
Huzhou • Ningbo
Hangzhou

Mianyang Three Gorges Dam • Wuhan
Chengdu Wanxian *Yangtze* Yueyang *East China*
• Nanchong *Dongting Hu* Nanchang *Sea*
Poyang Hu Wenzhou
• Chongqing Changsha
Neijiang • Pingxiang Fuzhou
Leshan
• Zigong
TAIWAN

Yalong Jiang
• Lapanshui • Yongzhou
• Guiyang • Shantou

Guangzhou • Shezhen
• Kunming Nanning • Hong
• Yulin Kong
Beihai • Zhanjiang

Jinsha Jiang

South China Sea

Hainan

0	500 miles
0	1000 km

Japan: Nuclear power

Nuclear energy is created when atoms of a nuclear fuel called uranium are split open to release lots of heat. The heat boils water and creates steam that powers turbines to make electricity. Most nuclear power stations are built by rivers or seas so they can use water from these sources to cool the steam.

Japan has few natural energy resources and has to import 80 per cent of its fuel. In the past, it relied totally on fossil fuels, which it imported mainly from the Middle East, but today 30 per cent of its electricity is generated in nuclear power stations. Nuclear power is suitable for Japan because the country consists of four islands, so there is a large amount of coastline that has easy access to water for cooling steam.

Nuclear power plants only require imports of relatively small amounts of uranium fuel. Building on flat land along the coast keeps power stations well away from the mountainous earthquake zones inland. If nuclear power stations are damaged there is a danger that cancer-causing radiation will escape into the air.

Japan is also developing more sustainable and safer energy sources. There are hydroelectric power plants, and geothermal plants are also being built. These tap into the underground hot water and steam created by the country's many volcanoes (see page 23).

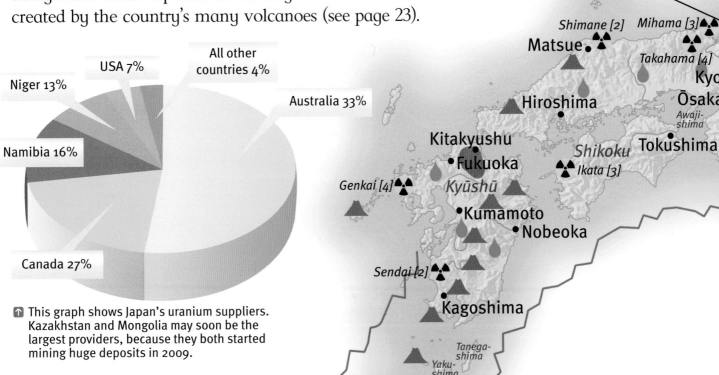

⬆ This graph shows Japan's uranium suppliers. Kazakhstan and Mongolia may soon be the largest providers, because they both started mining huge deposits in 2009.

Pie chart labels:
- Australia 33%
- Canada 27%
- Namibia 16%
- Niger 13%
- USA 7%
- All other countries 4%

Map labels:
- Sea of Japan
- Shika
- Tsuruga [2]
- Fugen
- Mihama [3]
- Shimane [2]
- Matsue
- Takahama [4]
- Kyoto
- Ōsaka
- Ohi
- Awaji-shima
- Hiroshima
- Kitakyushu
- Fukuoka
- Shikoku
- Tokushima
- Ikata [3]
- Genkai [4]
- Kyūshū
- Kumamoto
- Nobeoka
- Sendai [2]
- Kagoshima
- Tanega-shima
- Yaku-shima

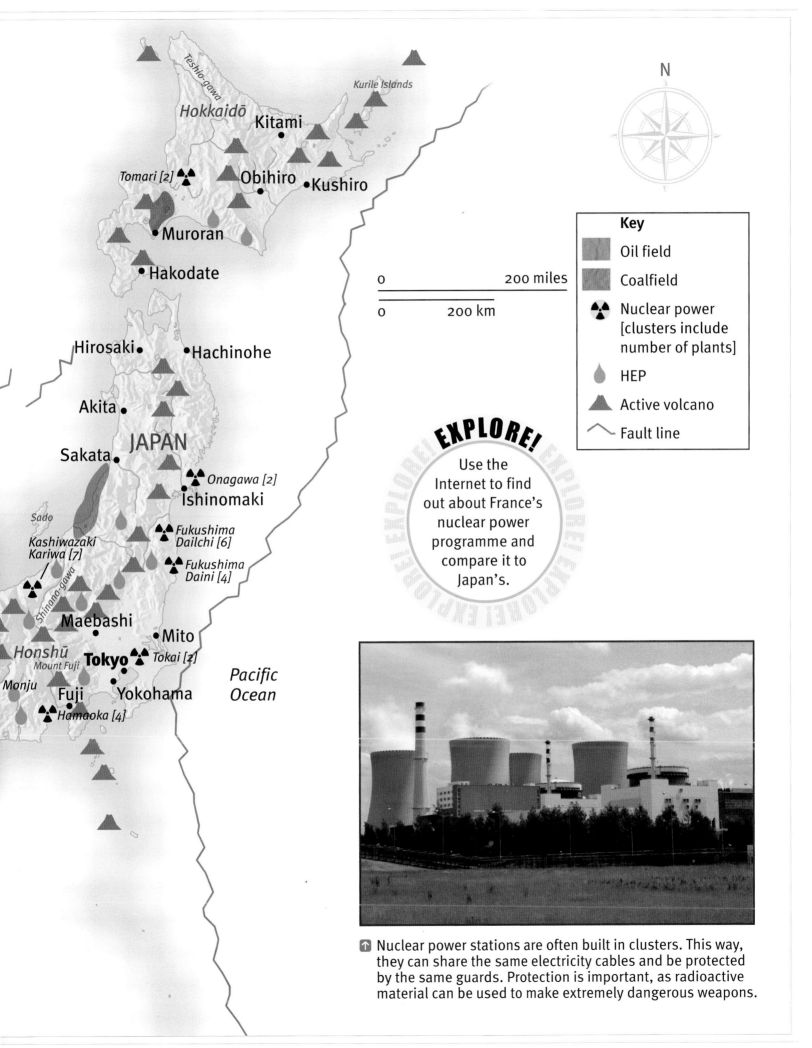

Hokkaidō

Kitami

Kurile Islands

Tomari [2]

Obihiro •Kushiro

•Muroran

•Hakodate

Hirosaki• •Hachinohe

Akita•

JAPAN

Sakata•

Sado

Onagawa [2]

Ishinomaki

Kashiwazaki Kariwa [7]

Fukushima Dailchi [6]

Fukushima Daini [4]

Maebashi

•Mito

Honshū Tokai [2]

Mount Fuji **Tokyo**

Monju

Fuji Yokohama

Hamaoka [4]

Pacific Ocean

N

| 0 | 200 miles |

| 0 | 200 km |

Key

Oil field

Coalfield

Nuclear power [clusters include number of plants]

HEP

Active volcano

Fault line

EXPLORE!

Use the Internet to find out about France's nuclear power programme and compare it to Japan's.

⬆ Nuclear power stations are often built in clusters. This way, they can share the same electricity cables and be protected by the same guards. Protection is important, as radioactive material can be used to make extremely dangerous weapons.

Australia: Uranium mining

One kilogram of uranium can produce as much energy as 1.5 million kilograms of coal. Unfortunately, huge amounts of ore have to be mined to get quite small amounts of uranium, so large areas of the natural landscape are devastated by the mining operations.

⬆ Olympic Dam Mine in south Australia is on the world's biggest deposit of uranium ore.

Australia has the largest uranium ore deposits in the world. These are located by the coast, so they can be easily exported by ship to other countries, including Japan. Australia supplies its own energy needs without nuclear power, so it doesn't have to process ore into highly radioactive fuel for power stations to use, or dispose of dangerous nuclear waste.

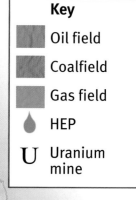

Key

- Oil field
- Coalfield
- Gas field
- 💧 HEP
- U Uranium mine

Darwin

U Ranger Mine

Townsville

Tanami Desert

Mount Isa

Great Sandy Desert

Port Headland

Alice Springs

Ashburton River

Gibson Desert

AUSTRALIA

Little Sandy Desert

Warrego River

Great Victoria Desert

Brisbane

U Olympic Dam Mine   U Beverly Mine

Barwon River

Bogan River

Darling River

Lachlan River

Perth

| 0 | 500 miles |
| 0 | 1000 km |

Newcastle
Sydney

Adelaide

Canberra

Melbourne

Tasmania

Hobart

Australia uses mainly coal, oil and gas energy sources. There are also hydroelectric power stations in the south-east, where there is abundant water. Australia has the potential to use more wind, solar and tidal energy but these are not being developed yet.

New Zealand:
Geothermal energy

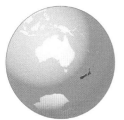

Geothermal energy uses natural heat from beneath the Earth's surface to make electricity. Most geothermal resources are in places where there are active volcanoes.

New Zealand is a good location for geothermal power stations because it has many hot, volcanic rocks and hot springs that can produce geothermal energy. Around 10 per cent of New Zealand's total energy is geothermal and the rest comes from hydropower, coal and gas stations. More geothermal plants, some solar and wind power are planned.

Key
- Oil field
- Coalfield
- Gas field
- HEP
- Wind power
- Volcanic area
- Hot spring area

Auckland

Waikato

Wanganui

Lake Taupo

Lake Waikaremoana

Rangitikei

Ngaruroro • Hastings

• Palmerston North

• Wellington

NEW ZEALAND

Buller

Awatere

Grey

Clarence

Lake Brunner

Waimakariri

Christchurch •

Rakaia

Ashburton

Lake Pukaki

Lake Wanaka

Pacific Ocean

Waitaki

Taieri

Lake Wakatipu

Lake Te Anau

Lake Manapouri

Dunedin •

Pomahaka

Lake Hauroko

⬆ Geothermal energy plants are much smaller than most other kinds of power station, and they don't pollute the air. They just release steam.

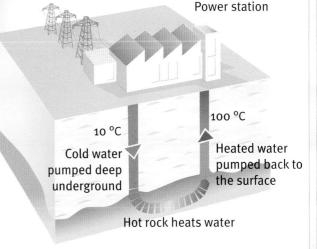

Power cables transmitting electricity to the national power grid

Power station

10 °C

Cold water pumped deep underground

100 °C

Heated water pumped back to the surface

Hot rock heats water

⬆ Geothermal energy plants can provide heating for buildings, as well as generate the electricity that these buildings need.

0 ___ 175 miles

0 ___ 250 km

North America:
Hydroelectric power

Hydroelectric power (HEP for short) is generated by damming big rivers. The stored river water turns electricity generators built inside the dams.

Most HEP stations in the USA are on rivers in the mountainous western states. The Hoover Dam, built in 1936, was one of the first HEP stations. Today, it supplies electricity to 1.3 million people in cities including Las Vegas. Canada is the world's largest HEP producer. Most of its HEP stations are along the St Lawrence Seaway in the east.

← The Hoover Dam created a new lake. It is called Lake Mead, after the engineer responsible for building the dam.

HEP supplies just 11 per cent of electricity generated in the USA, but over 60 per cent in Canada. The rest of North America's power comes mainly from fossil fuel and nuclear energy. Canada is also a major exporter of fossil fuel. HEP is not the region's only form of sustainable energy. Two out of three of North America's solar power plants are in sunny California and most of Canada's wind farms are near the windy Atlantic coast.

Arctic Ocean

Alaska (USA)

Northwest Territories

•Anchorage

Yukon Territory

Rocky Mountains

British Columbia

Hawai'i (USA)

Honolulu

Vancouver•

Washington

Seattle •

Oregon

Pacific Ocean

California *Nevada*

San Francisco•

Sacramento•

Las Vegas
Hoover Dam

Los Angeles

EXPLORE!

Find out about the negative impacts HEP stations have on the environment and in what ways they are environmentally friendly. Do you think that more countries should invest in HEP?

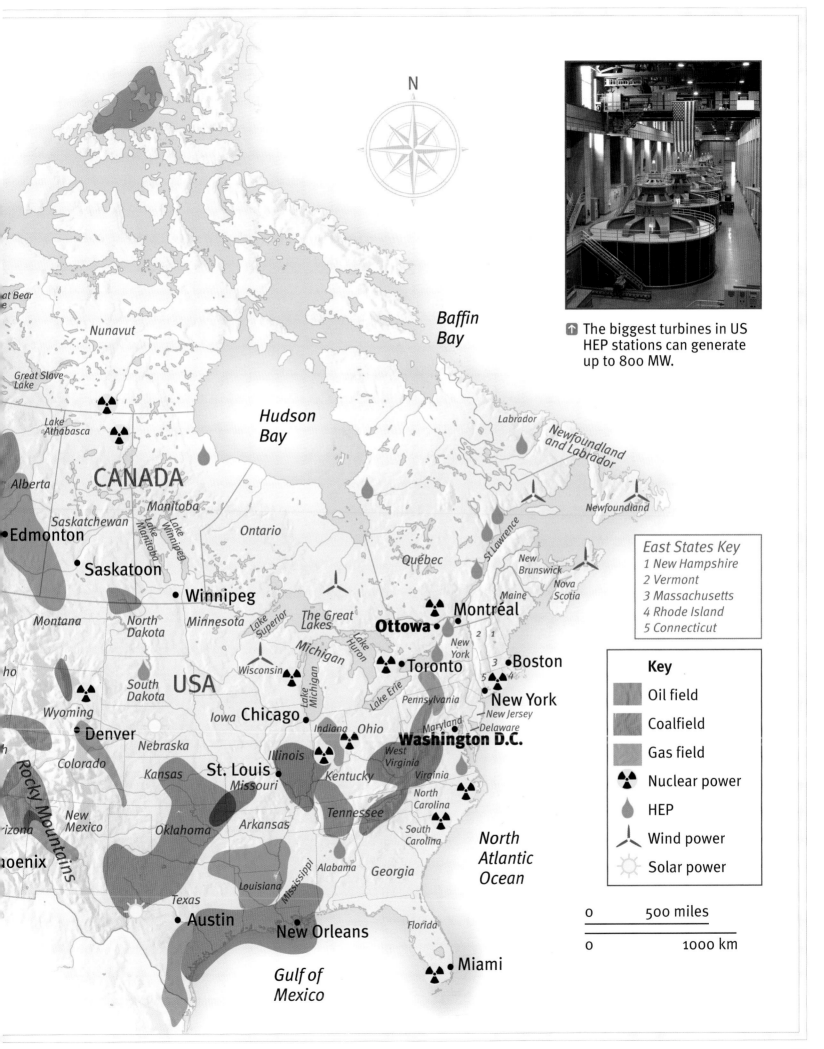

The biggest turbines in US HEP stations can generate up to 800 MW.

Baffin Bay

Hudson Bay

Nunavut

Great Slave Lake

Lake Athabasca

CANADA

Alberta

Edmonton

Saskatoon

Saskatchewan

Manitoba

Lake Winnipeg

Lake Manitoba

Winnipeg

Ontario

Labrador

Newfoundland and Labrador

Newfoundland

Québec

St Lawrence

New Brunswick

Nova Scotia

Ottowa

Montréal

Maine

Montana

North Dakota

Minnesota

Lake Superior

The Great Lakes

Lake Huron

Wisconsin

Lake Michigan

USA

South Dakota

Wyoming

Denver

Nebraska

Colorado

Kansas

Iowa

Chicago

Indiana

Ohio

Illinois

St. Louis

Missouri

Kentucky

Tennessee

Toronto

New York

Boston

New York

Lake Erie

Pennsylvania

New Jersey

Maryland

Delaware

Washington D.C.

West Virginia

Virginia

North Carolina

South Carolina

North Atlantic Ocean

New Mexico

Arizona

Oklahoma

Arkansas

Mississippi

Alabama

Georgia

Louisiana

Texas

Austin

New Orleans

Florida

Miami

Gulf of Mexico

Rocky Mountains

Phoenix

Idaho

at Bear

East States Key
1 New Hampshire
2 Vermont
3 Massachusetts
4 Rhode Island
5 Connecticut

Key
Oil field
Coalfield
Gas field
Nuclear power
HEP
Wind power
Solar power

| 0 | 500 miles |
| 0 | 1000 km |

Brazil: Ethanol production

Ethanol is a colourless, alcohol liquid. It is produced mainly from sugar cane, a crop that grows best in very warm, wet places. This is why central and south-eastern Brazil are the main sugar cane growing areas in South America.

Ninety per cent of Brazil's main electricity supply comes from HEP and the rest from fossil fuels. Oil for transport, however, used to have to be imported from the Middle East. Then, in the early 1970s, the price of oil from the Middle East rose suddenly and this encouraged scientists to invent a cheaper, alternative fuel – ethanol. By making use of its climate and land to grow sugar cane on huge plantations, Brazil became the second largest producer of ethanol in the world and no longer has to import fuel.

To make ethanol, sugar cane is pressed to extract sugary syrup. Then yeast is added to the syrup to convert the sugar into ethanol. By 2010 Brazil had more than 10 million ethanol-powered vehicles. Also, nothing of the sugar cane plant is wasted, because after processing, its residue generates the heat and electricity needed to produce the ethanol.

Rio Negro

Rio Japurá

Amazon

Rio Juruá

Rio Purus

Amazon Basin

Rio Branco •

Chap

← The ethanol is stored in huge storage tanks before it gets distributed and exported. This is an ethanol plant in Pradópolis.

EXPLORE!

Investigate one negative impact that sugar cane plantations can have on the environment.

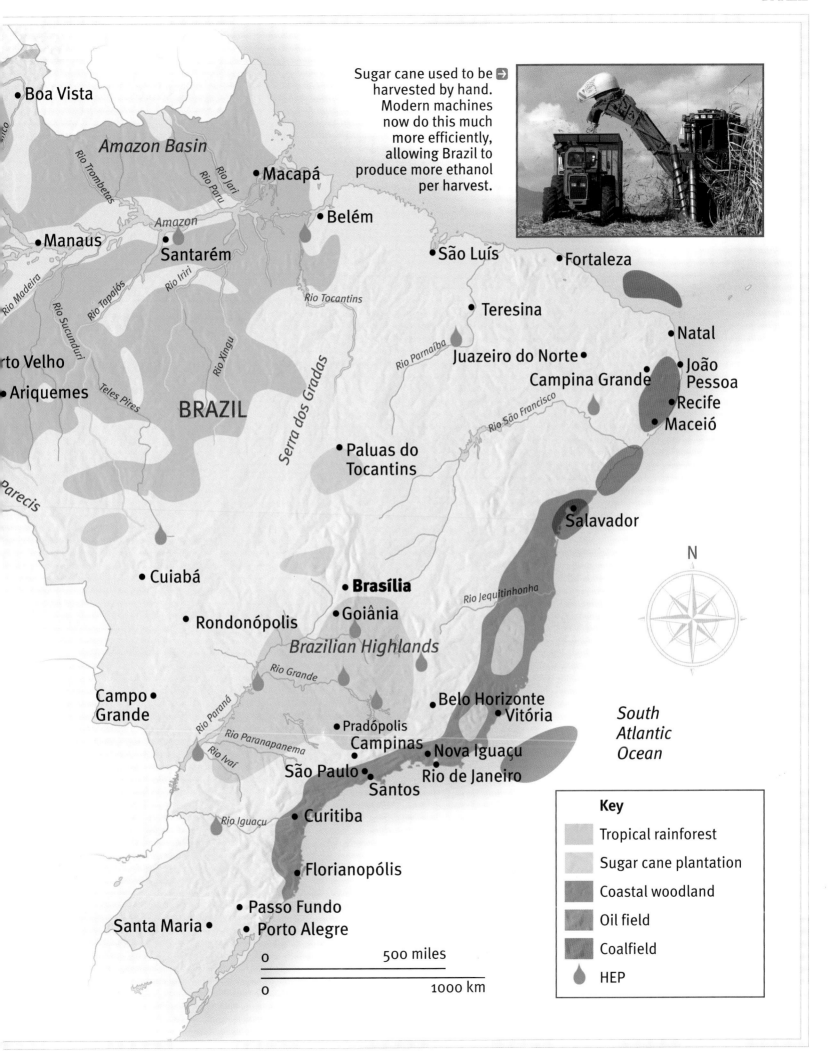

Sugar cane used to be ➡ harvested by hand. Modern machines now do this much more efficiently, allowing Brazil to produce more ethanol per harvest.

- Boa Vista

Amazon Basin

Rio Trombetas

Rio Jari

Rio Paru

- Macapá

Amazon

- Belém

- Manaus

- Santarém

Rio Iriri

Rio Madeira

Rio Tapajós

Rio Sucunduri

- São Luís

- Fortaleza

Rio Tocantins

- Teresina

to Velho

- Ariquemes

Teles Pires

Rio Xingu

BRAZIL

Serra dos Gradas

Rio Parnaíba

- Juazeiro do Norte

- Natal

- João Pessoa

- Campina Grande

- Recife

- Maceió

Rio São Francisco

Parecis

- Paluas do Tocantins

- Salavador

N

- Cuiabá

- Brasília

Rio Jequitinhonha

- Goiânia

- Rondonópolis

Brazilian Highlands

Rio Grande

Rio Paraná

- Campo Grande

- Belo Horizonte

- Vitória

South Atlantic Ocean

Rio Paranapanema

- Pradópolis

Rio Ivaí

- Campinas

- Nova Iguaçu

- São Paulo

- Rio de Janeiro

- Santos

Rio Iguaçu

- Curitiba

- Florianopólis

- Passo Fundo

- Santa Maria

- Porto Alegre

| 0 | 500 miles |
| 0 | 1000 km |

Key

- Tropical rainforest
- Sugar cane plantation
- Coastal woodland
- Oil field
- Coalfield
- HEP

Africa: Fuelwood

In African cities, most electricity comes from coal and some from HEP. However, more than half of all Africans live in the countryside – a long way from electricity supplies. Most people living in villages can only get heat for cooking and washing by gathering wood for fuel.

The map shows the areas where people have cut down so much fuelwood that the environment is being damaged by desertification. This is when land turns to desert because all the trees and plants that stopped soil in an area being worn away have been cut down. However, there are solar projects that could help villages that rely on fuelwood to get their energy sustainably.

⬆ Fuelwood is the main source of energy for cooking, washing and heating for most people living in African villages.

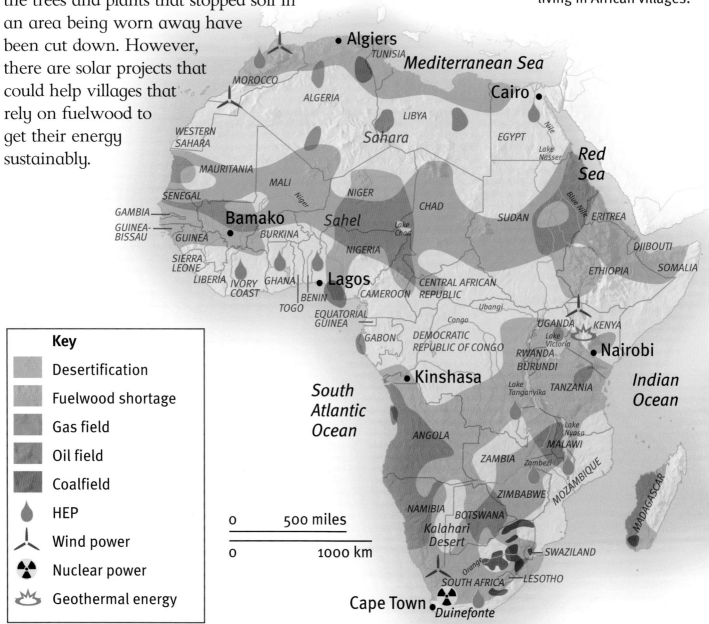

Key

	Desertification
	Fuelwood shortage
	Gas field
	Oil field
	Coalfield
⬤	HEP
⍲	Wind power
☢	Nuclear power
✸	Geothermal energy

0 ____ 500 miles
0 ____ 1000 km

Africa: Solar power

Solar power is obtained from the Sun's rays. The solar energy that falls on the Earth every year is over one thousand times the amount of energy used annually by every human being.

Generating solar power is one way of meeting Africa's growing energy needs. The generating equipment doesn't have any moving parts that could wear out quickly, and it doesn't use any fuel. Solar power is very environmentally friendly.

The map shows the parts of Africa that are ideal for generating solar power. It also shows which countries are either planning or have already installed solar power stations. Generating solar power is one way of meeting Africa's growing energy needs.

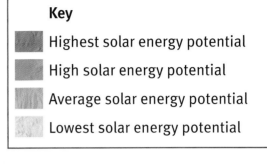

Key

	Highest solar energy potential
	High solar energy potential
	Average solar energy potential
	Lowest solar energy potential

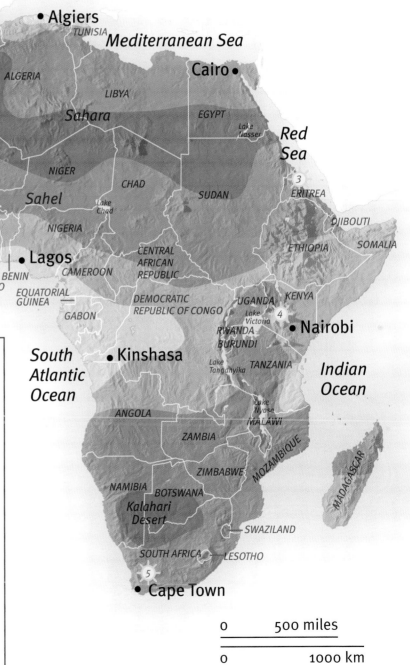

African Solar Projects

1. Morocco is planning to build a water desalination plant, which will use solar power to change seawater into freshwater.
2. Senegal supplies 10,000 homes in a remote coastal region with electricity generated from solar energy.
3. Eritrea has installed solar-powered water pumps to supply a number of villages with underground water.
4. Kenya uses solar power to provide electricity and heating for hospitals, schools and village health centres.
5. South Africa has completed a solar-powered water heating system which provides hot water to the 200 houses of a remote village.

Now test yourself!

These questions will help you to revisit some of the information in this book. To answer the questions, you will need to use the contents on page 2 and the index on page 32, as well as the relevant pages on each topic.

1 Use the contents on page 2 to find which pages show a map of:

(a) Russia's gas reserves.

(b) Japan's nuclear power stations.

(c) Australia's uranium mines.

2 Use the index on page 32 to find the answers to the following questions:

(a) What is the name of France's only tidal power station?

(b) Who is the world's largest producer and user of coal?

(c) Which crop produces most of Brazil's ethanol fuel?

3 Use the glossary to complete a copy of this table:

Key word	Meaning of this word
Generate	
	Fuel for nuclear power stations
Mining	
	A group of wind turbines

4 Use page 4 to explain how the Tata Nano car could change Asia's need for fuel energy.

5 Use page 6 to list the three types of fossil fuel and find out why they are all finite resources.

6 Use page 8 to explain how wave power is different from tidal power.

7 How does Australia meet some of Japan's fuel energy needs? The information on pages 20–22 will help you answer this question.

8 Which kinds of power station are shown in photographs A–C?

A  B   C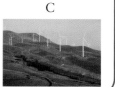

9 Use different pages in the book to explain how rocks and what happens under the Earth's surface can affect:

(a) where there are oilfields and gas fields.

(b) where it is safe to build nuclear power stations.

(c) where people could use geothermal energy.

10 What are the advantages (good things) and disadvantages (problems) about each of these sources of energy:

(a) coal?

(b) geothermal energy?

(c) nuclear power?

(d) wind power?

🌍 Glossary

biomass energy produced from burning plants and animal waste

climate change changes in the world's weather patterns caused by human activity

desertification the word used to describe the spread of the world's deserts

energy power produced by burning natural resources such as coal and using renewable alternatives such as wind power

ethanol a type of fuel produced from plant material such as sugar cane

field a large area where there are important energy resources, such as a coalfield

finite resources resources which will run out at some time in the future

fossil fuels sources of energy (like coal, oil and gas) formed from plants and animals which died millions of years ago

generate to produce electricity

geothermal energy a type of energy produced by heat from underground volcanic activity

global warming the increasing temperature of the Earth's atmosphere

greenhouse effect the warming effect on the atmosphere of burning fossil fuels. This is one cause of global warming

hydroelectric power (HEP) electricity generated by river or reservoir water flowing through turbines

mining digging materials such as coal and uranium from out of the ground

resources materials such as rocks, soil and water used to meet people's needs

pipeline a pipe used to transport large amounts of oil or gas

pollution damage caused to the natural environment by people's activities

power station a building where electricity is generated

solar energy electricity generated using the Sun's rays

sustainable resources resources which need not run out in the future if they are used wisely

tidal power electricity generated using the sea's high and low tides

uranium a metal used as the fuel for nuclear power stations

wave power electricity generated from the movement of waves on the surface of the sea

wind farm a group of wind turbines which can generate electricity

Index

First published in 2011 by Wayland
Copyright © Wayland 2011

Wayland
Hachette Children's Books
338 Euston Road
London NW1 3BH

Wayland Australia
Level 17/207
Kent Street
Sydney, NSW 2000

All rights reserved.

Editor: Julia Adams
Designer: Rob Walster, Big Blu Design
Cover design: Wayland
Map Art: Martin Sanders
Illustrations: Andy Stagg
Picture research: Kathy Lockley/Julia Adams

The website addresses (URLs) included in this book were valid at the time of going to press. However, it is possible that contents or addresses may have changed since the publication of this book No responsibility for any such changes can be accepted by either the author or the Publisher.

British Library Cataloguing in Publication Data
Gillett, Jack.
  Maps of the environmental world.
  Energy resources.
  1. Power resources--Environmental aspects--Juvenile literature. 2. Power resources--Environmental aspects--Maps for children.
  I. Title II. Gillett, Meg.
  333.79-dc22

ISBN 978 0 7502 6090 9

Printed in Malaysia

Wayland is a division of Hachette Children's Books, an Hachette UK company.
www.hachette.co.uk

Picture acknowledgements:
All photography: Shutterstock, except: p. 8: Maher/Sygmal/Corbis; p. 9: Wikimedia Commons; p. 16: Joerg Boethling/Still Pictures; p. 26: Brazilphotos.com/Alamy; p. 28: iStock

Maps of the Environmental World

Contents of titles in the series:

WAYLAND